WILDEBEEST

by

Gloria Samuel

Published by new Generation Publishing in 2023,
Copyright © Gloria Samuel 2023

First Edition

The author asserts the moral right under the Copyright, Designs and Patent Act 1988 to be identified as the author of this work.

All rights reserved. No part of this publication may be reproduced, stored in a retrieval system or transmitted, in any form or by any means without the prior consent of the author, nor be otherwise circulated in any form of binding or cover other than that which it is published and without a similar condition being imposed on the subsequent purchaser.

ISBN

Paperback 978-1-83563-115-7

www.newgeneration-publishing.com

Contents

The Wildebeest 1

The Gorilla Story 9

THE WILDEBEEST

He was a deceitful wildebeest; he had occupied a lot of grazing land by cunning means, from other beasts in the area of the port. The Port had fresh water, a prime location for migrating animals to relax in. Not forgetting human fishing and holiday makers.

He would often remind his fellow animals, that the pink pigs, once occupied the area in the 60's, whilst the black pigs took flight deep in jungles, when they could not fend off the pink pigs. The pink pigs were brutal and merciless. They eat everything in sight. Most of the animals in that area were herbivorous and ate only grass and shrubs.

All the pigs however, eat everything in sight. It didn't matter what; they ate worms, snakes, grasshoppers, rats, wild cats, dead dogs, flies, beetles, aphids. You name it, the pigs ate it. Because of this all the animals, took flight and hidden themselves deep in the jungle, with the gorillas.

He alone, was the only male wildebeest in the area, with his 2 wives and 4 wildebeest children. They occupied the region. The pigs were afraid of the wildebeest, because of their large horns and height.

Two of his children were from one wife and the other two, were from the other wife. Well! He only married one wife, and lived with the other wife from time to time.

In times pass, he would often boast to the sheep's of the area saying. 'Before the pigs came and drove all the other animals out. I have always had two money makers, whilst the other animals only had one'. He was referring to making babies with his wives.

As time went by, there were no more insects or small animals in the area to eat. Except mosquitoes, which the pigs hated, as they would jump on their backs and suck their blood.

Thus! The wildebeest and his family were the only animals in the area, and the mosquitoes hovered around the great river in the port, buzzing all day long, and suck their blood at night. The wildebeest were immune to the deadly malaria, because they kept chickens on their farm.

The male wildebeest then said to his wives. The animal's who took off into the jungle with the gorillas. Will soon return, they will need land to graze and fresh green grass to eat; as the jungle will be too harsh for them.

When they return I will pretend to sell them the land, after all they all ran away because of the pigs; and as they say in wars, 'to the victor goes the spoils'. 'I am the only one who stayed with my wives and 4 children.

However he placed a clause, in the land purchase, allowing all the returning animals to believe, that the land was theirs, to occupy fully as they feel; for a small portion of their grass land. What we humans call a (fee). The animals were all happy; think that they had gotten a bargain. Everyone loves bargain even animals.

The wildebeest then allowed all the animals to live on the land, near enough free of charge. Then one day as they were all grazing and enjoying themselves, with the nearly free grazing food pasture.

At a certain time of the year, the lions were doing their migration tour; cutting through the port area, to get from one city to the other. 'Lovely pasture' the lions cried out to the other animal, as they passed by.

Yes, replied the lambs to the lions, our brother the wildebeest, drove off the pigs from our land, and has allowed us to eat as much as we can, for nearly next to nothing, just for a nominal grass fee.

No, no, no, said the lions, there are no more fee paying land in the port area. The wildebeest, has tricked all of you. He has held on to all the land for himself and has made you to pay a grazing fee. (rent) but all the land is still his.

The lions said, a law has been passed, in the jungle courts. All animal must get a free hold 'title deed', to claim the full rights, to their portion of land. As times pass, the animals took the wildebeest to court. The king of the jungle court, found the wildebeest and his family, guilty of charges of deception. Allowing the animals to believe that the land was theirs, but in reality, the land belonged to the wildebeest and his family.

The king of the jungle had already passed a law over 20 years ago. That all animals in the jungle must get a freehold title deed; at the expense of the wildebeest, providing proof that land is theirs.

The wildebeest and his family were quite upset over the verdict of the court but there was nothing he could do. All the animals then said it's been over 50 human years. We have been paying him, the wildebeest nominal grazing fees.

The jungle court then said to the wildebeest, you've taken enough grazing fees, for pastoral grazing from your fellow animals, for the last 50 years.

The court orders the wildebeest, to cut all the animals a freehold title deed, and register them all at the jungle administration land office.

THE GORILLA STORY

Woke up got dress with a spring in my steps I said to myself. Today I am going to write myself a child's book.

There was a gorilla who decided to marry a chimpanzee. Because he the gorilla could not get away from the chimpanzee no matter how he tried. He even travelled as far as Europe in a cage; to London zoo but he couldn't get away from the chimps their either.

He behaved so badly at London zoo, sleeping with one chimpanzee after the next, making 32 babies. The zoo keepers had a meeting and decided to ship him back to Africa.

On arrival in Africa, they all thought that he would settle down in the jungle. After all he was home, 'but did he settle down boys and girl'. No! He did not. All he did was wondered about in the jungle, sniffing trees, to see if female chimpanzees were around.

He smelt out so many lady chimpanzees against the trees, and immediately knew he had his full choice. Ha! He said to himself, I am a man gorilla and I have been to London zoo. I know I can have my pick, of lady chimps, now that I'm home. I am like a king here in gorilla paradise. One day his gorilla playmates called and asked him why does he not choose a gorilla to wife and have children. Why does he want to play with chimpanzees?

He the Gorilla replied and said to his male friends. Because whilst at London zoo. I had a lot of female gorilla's lady friends and I made 32 children with them. They gave me a lot of grief, which made me, behave so bad, the zoo keeper said, it was bad for my mental health, and decided to ship me back to Africa.

Now that I am here, I no longer wishing to have female gorilla friends, but chimpanzee's female friends, easier to tame. Ok his friend said, we now understand. bye, bye, have a nice day.

After sniffing a number of trees and finding a chimpanzee that pleased him. He decided to settle down with her and have some babies. However he soon got bored with her, because there weren't enough tricks, up her sleeves to please him and keep him occupied.

So he started wondering off in the jungles of Africa again. This time he met a very cunning and sly chimpanzee; one that matched him. He then left his chimpanzee wife. Whom he had made a few monkeys with, and married this new chimpanzee. She was a terror an extraordinary chimp.

She had mingled, with the stars of chimpanzee land; that had arrived from all around the world. As a matter of fact, she was adopted from a very young age of 6, by a male pig, from a UK farm in Plymouth. Who had temporarily relocated to Africa during the early 1960's.

She had everything she needed but the pig who had adopted her. Was very strict, and a bit of a devil bag. When she the chimpanzee went to bed at night; he would creep into her cage, which was left open each night and fiddle with her money maker; that she kept under her skirt. It became the pig's habit to jump in her cage, when he felt like and she couldn't do anything about it.

After all she was getting the fame and adulations from all the other animals, which were living far beneath her status, but if anyone knew what the pig from Plymouth was doing, most nights; creeping into her cage then into her money maker and stealing her provisions. It would be a shame on him. So the chimpanzee put up with the pig's DISGUSTING behaviour for years. Until the pig was finally called by his bosses and shipped back to the farm in Plymouth. He was on a fact finding mission.

By now, she the chimpanzee was so famous, that everyone in the village knew her, so when the gorilla from London zoo, came along. He was impressed at her vast antics she had acquired from the pig. When the gorilla asked her questions, she knew the answer. There was no question she could not answer or find out about.

The gorilla then decided to marry lady chimpanzee. The entire marriage was so upsetting for the new chimpanzee bride. That she speaks of it to date. She tells everyone who would listen. She said that her rival chimpanzee. Whom she had stolen the gorilla from, made her wear her cast-off wedding garment, on the day of her wedding, as a punishment for stealing the gorilla, from his first chimpanzee wife and children.

Although they eventually reconciled, it serves as a bad memory to the new chimpanzee bride. Following on from the wedding of Mr Gorilla and Miss Chimpanzee, they had many optical thrown in their path.

The Gorillas in London zoo with their 32 children; was harassing them in spirit with jungle drum cries. Which they could physically hear with their special jungle echo hearing sounds.

When it wasn't the female gorilla sounds they heard. It was the sounds of his 32 gorilla children, harassing him in spirit, to return to London zoo, to take care of them.

When she was finally able to block out the echo sounds from London zoo. They were harassed by the local chimpanzees in Africa, whom he had left to marry the current chimp.

How was she able to keep him until death when they parted? She got him so excited and worked up, built them a beautiful tree house; that other chimpanzees, came and paid them in peanuts and bananas. To stay a few nights in the big tree house, just to hear their stories. This made the Gorilla very happy and popular in the local area. A local superstar with everyone, he had finally become somebody of stature.

One day he became board and restless, curious took him into the jungle. There he started his old habit of, sniffing out other chimpanzees to play with. By now he and Mrs Chimpanzee had given birth to three monkeys and their tree house was making them good money.

He located his old friends in the jungle that he had left to become famous. Well he didn't leave them to become famous. He left because of manipulation, love and seduction. However he soon fell back into his old habit. He started playing with other female chimpanzees and went inside their money makers.

Well the girls in the jungle didn't mind when he came around. Because he bought with him lots of peanuts and bananas for them and their children. Especially the girls whose husbands, had left them with the children alone. They entertained the gorilla at his leisure.

By now Mrs Chimpanzee in the capital city, was fuming with rage and anger; which landed straight in the centre of her heart and in her mind. She was like 'the jungle, has no fury than a chimpanzee scorned'. Her anger plagued her. Then one day a male friend, who visited the tree house regularly. Said to her, the only way to shake your anger and even up the score is to do the very same thing.

Going into the jungle as advised and playing with the purse of another gorilla. The female chimpanzee felt satisfied. She had finally got her revenge.

When her gorilla husband, heard what she had done. He decided to leave her but he couldn't. Because of their fame and the big tree house, they had built in town. So instead of saying to him, we're now even.

Mr. Gorilla was so elevated in the community. He decided to spite his wife, the female chimpanzee; but he didn't know what to come up with.

By now his first monkey daughter was about 15 years old. She ate a lot of red-berries every 28 days; she was very beautiful. His gorilla friends advised him, to go into his daughter's cage at nights and shake her money maker. After that he would feel at peace; and his rage against his chimpanzee wife would leave him. He did as his friend advised him, and before you know what had happened boys and girl. His monkey daughter was pregnant, with a son by her gorilla father. He also had another daughter, he was doing the same thing to, but she never get pregnant by her gorilla father. It then became the family's open secret.

The word got around and everyone in town; knew that the new orangutan was born, as a product from his monkey daughters and her gorilla father.

It was a secret because there was a law in the jungle that says. Gorilla that gives birth to monkeys via a chimpanzee must not trouble the money maker of the monkeys and give birth to Orangutans.

They then all lived with the curse of the orangutan in their lives. They loved him he was theirs. The gorilla father; was happy about the birth of the orangutan. He had developed an insatiable rage against his chimpanzee wife, which had now cooled down.

He said to himself, this is now bone of my bone and flesh of my flesh. She ate red-buries every 28 days and I am the only one, who went in her cage and troubled her money maker, thus producing my first orangutan. However, the orangutan was kept hidden by the family. It was against the laws of the jungle; to do such an abominable thing in the entire jungle. What happened to orangutan? Well, that's another story boys and girls.

Milton Keynes UK
Ingram Content Group UK Ltd.
UKHW022009110324
439294UK00005B/64